Blooms,
Blunders, and Blessings

To Red and Lori,

Thanks so much! I
enjoyed our visit, and
look forward to hearing
what you think of this
book.

Good health and God's
Blessing,

Marjorie Vaughn Eldred

Blooms, Blunders, and Blessings

Blooms, Blunders, and Blessings

Garden Stories I Just Had to Tell

Revised and Expanded

Second Edition

Marjorie Vaughn Eldred
Contributions by
Mona Armas
Douglas L. Skelton

Blooms, Blunders, and Blessings

Copyright @2011, 2014
By Marjorie Eldred

Golden Valley Gems
6403 241 Avenue East
Buckley, WA 98321

ISBN: 978-0-9849859-3-7

Printed in the United States of America

To Clio
My Most Faithful and
Enthusiastic Fan

Blooms, Blunders, and Blessings

Blooms, Blunders, and Blessings

Come to my garden. I have beauties to share, flowers, trees, woodlands.
I have nature's creatures that challenge my gardening efforts.
I will make you smile, I promise. You'll be glad you came.
Marjorie Eldred

"A garden should make you feel you've entered privileged space —a place not just set apart but reverberant —and it seems to me that, to achieve this, the gardener must put some kind of twist on the existing landscape, turn its prose into something nearer poetry."
Michael Pollan, *Second Nature: A Gardener's Education*

Blooms, Blunders, and Blessings

Table of Contents

Blooms, Blunders, and Blessings

Gardener's Prayer

Especially, I love the garden, Lord. I am not surprised that You chose a garden to place your first family in, or that You wanted them to tend it. What a perfect place to feel Your presence, to be reminded of Your love by the vibrant colors You placed there.

What a perfect way to learn responsibility, and the results of shirking it. Thank You for giving us trees and shrubs, vines and flowers. The garden allows and encourages creativity in the way the gardener chooses to arrange Your gifts, the flowers and shrubs. The garden provides respite and restoration to the weary of heart. What a gift is a garden!

We moved into a new home in August 2002. We're starting a new garden from scratch!

Garden Diary, 2004

I'm going back to the digging project. The ultimate intent is to make a larger front bed so I can put in some flowering trees and some kind of property-definition shrubs. We have a neighbor right in front of us now, and their windows to consider. I think they are planning to put in some rhododendrons along the front part of the border. That's exciting!! I'll probably go with roses. The two borders should work well together. It sure takes a lot of work to make a house into a home!!

May 2004: I went outside a little bit ago, and took two or three pictures of the yard. It seems to be developing nicely; not at all fancy, or professionally done, but pretty. The Astilbe are beautiful this year, and the blue hydrangea has lots of blooms, none of which are as dark blue as I wanted, but pretty, none the less. The Robin Hood rose has been absolutely stunning, but the blooms are fading now. We'll have to wait awhile for more.

The Easter-Lily bulbs I planted in the garden are just beginning to bloom. I planted additional bulbs this year that were given to me last March. It is so neat to know they will come back again, probably on their own schedule. I remember planting Easter Lilies in Wenatchee and having them bloom while the Chrysanthemums were blooming in the fall, the next year. Amazing, huh? I have pictures!

I am really enjoying our developing landscape. It seems to welcome us home whenever we've been away. I love watching everything grow, and there are some new plants in my garden this year demanding my attention. Mom and I planted some Zinnia and Snap-dragon seeds several weeks ago. Those will soon be ready to transplant, I bought a few more plants last week; some are perennials like Portulaca (moss rose). I also bought a few begonias with red leaves and blooms, and some Sweet-William.

Buying more plants locally is the sure sign that I will get whatever plants I have previously ordered from catalogs, and I'll get them immediately. This time it was Chrysanthemums. My work is cut out for me right now.

Saturday was a big day this week. I started cleaning in the house, then Clio told me that Bob, our angel in blue jeans, was coming up to help clean out the sink drains. Maybe, too, he would help set up the Sunsetter awning that has been lying in the garage for months. Bob came. He and I worked all afternoon on the awning, timing the outside stuff between rain showers; retreating to shelter, studying instructions while we waited.

Bob got the awning up. It really looks nice, and creates a new room for us. Right now, the way the weather is, I must leave it tilted to one corner so the rain can drain. The neighbors may think we should have had a professional put it up.

August 2004: Some time ago I ordered a Compost Tumbler to help me build up the poor soil in our landscape—a lot of plants aren't growing as they should, but are turning yellow. The tumbler came today, so I'm waiting for Clio to get around so he can help me put it together. While he is plugging away at getting dressed, I am out cutting blackberry vines—the very first berries are ripening!

The visiting doe stood about twenty-five or thirty feet from our back windows, right in front of the berm. As Mom said, she was looking right at us. Mom called me away from my book, I called Clio. The doe waited patiently for us to gather. She intended to dine and didn't want to leave until she had done so. I ran for my camera and took one picture. Clio said I should open the window so we could see better—at 9 P.M. it was almost dark. I tried for several more pictures—wishful thinking—while she stood there. Then she wandered over and offered to take another bite of my strawberry plants, and I ran for the deck where I waved my arms vigorously. At first she just looked at me, and then she wandered over behind the berm and headed toward the woods. In astonishment we watched her stop, turn around and return to the far side of the berm where she'd obviously enjoyed my Autumn Joy Sedum plant before. Wanting to prevent any more damage I waved my arms wildly and added a few sound effects. She was not afraid of us, not a little. I took off across the grass, wanting to frighten her away. Finally she moseyed down the path, definitely taking her own sweet time, and disappeared into the woods.

All this time Clio talked about how fat she was and how good she'd be to eat. He said he'd have to get a hunting license—I don't think he'd ever get permission to fire a real gun from our yard; he's already done some target practice with a pellet gun.

Last night I said I wouldn't want to eat her, but this morning when I went out and found some of my new carnation plants chomped off and pulled out of the ground, I changed my mind. At the moment I'm not so sure Clio's idea isn't a good one.

Mom says I should spray my plants with soap suds to keep the deer away. I don't know. She may be right, and perhaps I will try it.

October 2004: This week I planted at least eighty Perennial Tulip bulbs, replacements for the bulbs I put in a large pot in the garage last year and lost. I bought them from Springhill. That company is really good about sending replacement plants or bulbs if *anything* ever happens that you are not enjoying the plants you purchased. Fool proof, you might say. They never charge you again.

We've had one or two days nice enough to get outside and work. I've finally planted my tiny Arbor Society flowering trees–Crab apples and Dogwoods. I feel happy to have them in the ground and look forward to spring and watching them grow. It will be quite a while before they look like trees; they measure about two feet tall now. I also planted a little tree—name unknown—that I got the day I went to help Doug in his yard. It is only about six inches tall. Nothing like planting for the future, is there? I guess the way to bring the reality into existence is to dream.

The tulips, iris, and alliums are all in the ground now, too. What I need to do next is buy a load of bark and get it spread. I've done so much digging that weeds will be an awful problem if I don't get it done.

November, 2004: My pile of bark is still much too large. We unloaded it between our driveway and the neighbor's. When it rains, water stands around it and looks awful. I hope Dick and Patty aren't too bothered by it. Maybe Wednesday afternoon I will be able to make further progress in spreading it around.

The moles are still driving me crazy. Dick sets traps occasionally. He's learned how to catch them, poor babies. I wish they would leave us alone so we could leave them alone.

November 2004: I've been making a little progress with spreading my bark one shovel full at a time. What frustrates me is that I spread the bark, then the moles push up through it, then I do the bark again. Ideally, it will keep most of the weeds down. I have a long way to go yet. The neighbors are commenting that the pile is going down—I'm glad they can see progress. I asked Dick if he'd want to use a little of it. Yeah! Every little bit helps. He has helped me in so many ways that it's nice to do something for him.

Oops! Somebody Goofed!

It must be my age that made me want a raised garden, or perhaps it was the constant struggle to plant in soil full of rocks and boulders, or maybe it was the grocery bill, ever growing with the economic down-turn.
I wanted to grow vegetables again.

I was motivated, too, by the appearance of the flower bed on the west side of the house. It had been beautiful for awhile with its lemon-thyme and yarrow inter-plantings. That was until the invasive nature of both of those plants became obvious and the grass started moving into the bed. This spring it was a mess, and the only solution was to start over. If I was going to start over, why not build a raised bed?

The memories of my previous success with squash, beans, and other great out-of-the-garden dinners we enjoyed moved me to ask my sons to help me. They intended to, they really did, but the one who actually helped most was our friend Bob, who had the experience, the tools, and the trailer to haul the lumber. Most-important, he had the time.

I didn't want a one-foot high garden. I couldn't help thinking how much it would help to have it two feet high. Just think how much easier the weeding, planting, and harvesting would be; hardly any bending would be necessary. The decrease in required effort would really help on the sun-beaten west side of the house.

Clio caught my enthusiasm and made it his job to check out availability and prices of lumber. He also made sure Bob knew we were building the garden, and that we would need some help; his help. Clio's son, Cyle, promised help as well.

When Bob knew he was going to be involved, he went about buying lumber, bolts, and metal stakes. He worked out of our sight in his garage, and one Friday morning he surprised me by appearing in our driveway with his trailer load of supplies. Bob is a man of few words. I greeted him and watched as he began to unload the building materials. Finally, I had to ask, "Are you planning to put the raised bed up today?"

"Yes," he answered. "It's not supposed to rain."

Bob had done all the preparatory work; cutting the lumber, drilling holes for the bolts, and cutting the iron staking to exact lengths, so the actual assembly was finished by noon. It looked great. My husband and our friend Bob had given me a wonderful gift, just in time for Mother's Day and my birthday. I was grateful. Bob went home, and I began to enjoy the possibilities in earnest. Now I actually had the raised bed. I could plant vegetables.

Saturday morning I was excited. My grown-up kids planned to spend the day with me. Mother's Day had just passed and my birthday was approaching. We were going to celebrate together. The work was all done on the garden bed, we thought, and we could ignore it and just enjoy one another. I wanted to share some of my writing projects, at least with my daughter.

At 9:30 the families began to arrive. The driveway filled with kids, grandkids, hugs, and sounds of happy voices. I walked around the garden with Doug, my son who loves gardening as much as I do.

As we came around from the back yard I was surprised to hear voices sounding not so happy. One of them was unfamiliar. One belonged to my husband.

"You can't have that in the side yard," I heard. "That isn't what we talked about." Our park manager stood outside the open bedroom window.

"It's exactly what I told you we wanted to do, and you said it would be okay in either our side or back yard," I heard Clio say.

We live in a park where all building projects must be approved by the manager.

"That's not what we agreed on. That garden's three feet high," the manager exaggerated.

"I told you it would be two feet high, and you're looking at a two foot bed," Clio tried again.

"You can't leave that there. If you start filling it, I'll come and cut it down myself, and charge you for it!"

When the manager saw me come around the house with questions on my face, he exploded. "I've had at least six neighbors call me. The garden has to come down! Clio's not listening to me."

Suddenly, a bright May morning turned gloomy. We thought this situation unbelievable since we had already notified him of our intentions and received his permission. He corrected us, in spite of the driveway full of cars and the presence of our family. He insulted us with his tone of voice and demeanor. He treated us like naughty children. He stole our happy day and replaced it with frustration.

After our discouraging visitor had gone home, my sons and Clio in his wheelchair gathered in the side yard discussing what to do next. But our troubles had just begun.

Our next door neighbor came out of the house and joined the discussion. We had previously shared our plans with him and asked about a two-foot raised bed there, and he had given his agreement. "I don't like it, and my wife doesn't like it. It's not what we expected!"

The day darkened. I did not witness the scene that followed, but both of my sons who were present reported it later.

When I went outside, shortly after the manager left, one son was livid. "Tell me where he lives. I'm going to let him know what I think of him! Tell me where he lives! Where does he live Mom? Which house is his?"

I did not tell him. Enough harm had been done.

Now we had to repair the situation if we could. Gary volunteered to go home and get his power saw that would cut the iron stakes. He left with a close friend of my daughter's. They were gone a long time. When they returned Gary looked for the saw in his car. No saw!

Apparently, he and Mark took time to relax and enjoy Gary's rebuilt car project, and consequently forgot *why* they had gone to his house! They sheepishly re-entered Gary's car and repeated the five mile trip, this time remembering the saw. This is one memory of that day we can smile about.

The job of reducing the bed height took about thirty minutes. The bolts had to be loosened, the stakes cut. What would we do with the extra lumber which had holes drilled in it? Another garden? No. The misunderstandings had stolen the joy from the first one.

We found the joy again. Now we are savoring the fruits of our labors, the harvest from our garden: yellow summer squash, tomatoes, cucumbers, beans. We are sharing them with our neighbors. I think I'll take tomatoes to the park manager.

I can remember where he lives now.

Garden Diary, 2005

January 2005: The flowers are growing! The bulbs are beginning to peek through. I've seen crocus and garlic, also possibly some allium and daffodils. Some of the day-lily plants are showing. I'm hoping the rest of them didn't die out.

I'm still working on the pile of bark. I cleaned out a previously ignored bed and covered it with bark last night. It's great to see the small improvements.

March 2005: I'm enjoying watching things come up; mostly, they are bulbs of one kind or another. Some of the perennial tulips I planted two years ago seem to be dividing, which probably means I didn't get them planted deep enough. I'll be able to dig them and replant, but it is so difficult to get anything planted *nine* inches deep that I don't know whether they will ever behave the way they are supposed to. There are so many large rocks! The perennial tulips were so beautiful the first year. I don't know if I can bear it if they don't keep blooming. I can't help remembering Wenatchee!

March 2005: Speaking of brambles: since the guys trimmed the blackberries in the back, I've been pulling dead vines out of the thicket, cutting them up, and piling them in our cleared area. I've found that they do not grow again after being cut and dried, but soon build a mulch layer that does a fair job of keeping weeds out. I'm thinking about planting a few vegetables this year in that area, so I'm trying to plan ahead for that, too. I may never get any of it done, but it's fun to think about eating fresh roasting ears, fresh beans, and cucumbers. Zucchini sells for nearly a dollar a pound, if you can believe that!

I have a wonderful time with the many seed and flower catalogues that come to my address. I didn't think about getting so many when I asked for an address or two for catalogues. Now it seems like every day I get a new catalogue or three. Unfortunately, I always find things I want and have a royal battle between me, myself, and I before deciding to stay within my budget and do without most of them.

Mom looks endlessly at the pictures and lets me know what she likes too. Tonight it was hydrangeas, red, white, and blue. I told her I had them in my garden; they just haven't bloomed yet. Over and over she told me about them. I never could convince her I already had them.

Later in March, 2005: I've figured out how to do a few lawn chores without breaking my bending, twisting rules. I missed a curve in Eastern Washington and the crash caused a compression fracture in my back. I can turn the front water faucet on by getting down on a piece of carpet and reaching. Judy turned the back water on today. I couldn't reach the faucet but needed to water the flowers in the back yard. Dick loaned me a long handled tool to cut out dandelions. My energy doesn't last long, so I don't *do* much of anything, but being out and busy helps me enjoy the yard a little more and not stress about everything I can't do. Lisle helped me plant my Kaliedescope Hydrangeas, and Bob helped plant another bunch of plants I had ordered. I have two new Hostas that I'm really excited to see. I am really learning to appreciate my neighbors.

April 2005: The neighbors continue to help out. Dick helped me unload a bag of rock chips, John helped mow the lawn, Judy helped again by turning the back water faucet on and off. Clio continues to help me in and out of my brace. I don't know what I'd do without any of them. I've been trying to find a landscape maintenance professional to help out on a more regular basis. Yard maintenance people are so hard to find because of the demand. They want about $35 to mow our lawn. I had a man come today to give me an estimate; we will probably know tomorrow. It would be nice if the insurance company didn't have a per-day limit.

May 2005: I lined up help with the yard work about ten days ago. It looks like I will be coming out okay on the insurance if I don't have them mow every week. They can help in the flower beds every other week; perhaps help me keep from falling too far behind. I am seeing so much that I would *like* to do and a lot that <u>has</u> to be done. Probably I will have to be happy with the necessary chores this year. Since a garden is a living, constantly developing thing, it's hard to watch needs being un-met. Green Effects—the name of the yard-maintenance service—has been here once to mow. This Thursday they will be back to help in the beds. Communicating is quite a challenge. The guys are both Spanish-speaking. One guy can communicate, but knows only a little about flowers. The other is an experienced gardener, but doesn't understand much, if any, English. It will be interesting.

The school district didn't allow me to go back to work. The doctor had written "light duty" on his permission slip, along with restrictions, and that was enough to make them over-cautious.

I drove to Auburn that morning, thinking I was going to work, believing that the doctor had sent the papers. He had not. I had to come home and make phone calls which in the end came to nothing. That's okay. I probably have enough to do without being away from home every day.

June 2005: Time disappears mysteriously these days. I'm not sure why but think it might have something to do with having to manage all the help I'm getting on the house and yard. Yard maintenance is scheduled for Thursday mornings. The guys mow the lawn this week, and other chores like weeding, digging, edging, will happen next week. They've been a huge help; the two men are here for one-half hour. Neither of them speaks much English. Thankfully, it turns out, the one that understands me the best also knows something about flowers, so he isn't likely to dig them out enthusiastically. I always have to get up early on Thursday mornings, since I'm never sure when they will be here. One day they didn't get here at all, and another it was noon. Usually they show up about nine A.M. I'm afraid that most Thursdays I greet them sans-make-up!

Doctor said I can get up without my brace!

July 2005: There's not too much going on in my garden. Only part of the beans I planted and only one corn plant has come up. I didn't realize how shady the spot stayed until after I planted the seeds. Just for fun, I buried some sprouted sweet potatoes this morning. If they come up, it'll be fun to see what they do. Several of the zinnia seeds I put close to the house have come up. I'll have to do some transplanting, but they are easy to do. I'll have to watch for slugs.

August 2005: Today I cut the last blooms off Siberia, the white, tall, very fragrant lily. Two blooms are in the house perfuming our environment. Siberia was in bloom for over two weeks. The next lily to bloom was Rosoto, also very tall, mostly white with pink highlights, and fragrant. It is still in bloom, as is Stargazer, a pink with red spots and white edged petals. Stargazer is shorter, but also perfumes the yard. Walking through the garden will be a treat for some time now, especially in the evening when the fragrance fills the air.

I am edging our rather long back yard path with red brick. It hasn't been as hard or as hot as I anticipated since I was able to work in the early-morning shade or on cloudy days, which seemed in ample supply to complete the job.

I got the bricks in Puyallup at River Road Landscaping. I made four trips and laid over two-hundred bricks. Most of the path is finished. I still plan to line the strawberry patch and around the composter.

My latest project has been getting a new tree planted to replace the small one the deer have been eating for their midnight snack. I bought a larger tree, a flowering cherry. Dick helped me get it out of the pot and hold it straight while I put the soil in and watered it. Then I hammered stakes into the ground to build a fence around the tree. As usual I kept hitting rock before the stakes were deep enough. I pounded three or four stakes in before I completely wilted. Bob came unexpectedly around the house and asked if I needed help. He drove the last stake and helped me put together a chicken wire fence to keep the deer away from the tree. I tied a lot of ribbon on the tree and fence, hoping the newness would discourage the deer. Then I added some spare CD's—Les's idea. So far, so good. I'm a little afraid if they get brave enough, the fence won't do any good at all.

They had nothing to do with it, but my kids inhabit my garden. Doug is a small boy on a log, busy investigating the inside of the log. Gary—the pitcher—and Tim—the catcher—are playing baseball. Barbara is watching fairies from a stump in the back yard. The little statues make me smile when I see them and remember my kids as children.

Also, in their hiding places in the front garden, are my three geeky beeks—jiggly long legged silly-looking birds with out-stretched necks. They move around from time to time with the help of the wind and my other visitors. Their present hiding places were inspired by my sister Mona.

September 2005: I'm battling the moles again. They've started coming up in the middle of the lawn and at the edges of the beds. Their favorite place seems to be under the bricks I just installed. My latest weapon—which either works marginally, or not at all—is juicy fruit gum. Here's the process. I shovel all the dirt off the lawn, pop the stick of gum in my mouth and chew it, dig down to find the mole tunnel, remove the gum from my mouth, throw it into the tunnel and cover up the whole mess. Theoretically the mole should chew the gum; it is supposed to upset his stomach and maybe he'll go to sleep forever—if we're lucky. I read the idea in one of those mail-out advertisements that give you just enough information to drive you crazy. The complete answer is in the book, of course. So far it seems to work about as well as anything else I've ever used.

I'm covering the tomato vine at night now. I haven't seen frost yet, but apparently it is too cold to successfully grow vegetables.

My spring veggies were planted in mid-July, and the squash has done well. I've been picking several zucchini each week; they are so good we've eaten them all. The beans are beginning to form, but probably will not continue to develop. The corn, mostly, did not come up; I wonder if I should have soaked the seeds.

I've been working on my next year's vegetable space by digging in all the kitchen and garden waste` except meat. I also add all the extra soil the moles bring to the surface. The new space gets twice as much sunshine as the space I planted in this year.

November 2005: Since the first of October I have received all the bulbs and plant starts I'd ordered during the summer. I need to remember when I'm ordering that nothing seems to arrive until the rains begin; the summer has gone and with it taken my desire to garden. I've managed to plant a few more tulips, hyacinths, and daffodils. I've planted a Beauty of Moscow Lilac—a pink one—a Flowering Almond bush, a Rose of Sharon, and a few more perennials, too. Queen of the Prairie, tall Phlox, and variegated iris should color up next summer's garden and give lots of new bloom to enjoy. Filling empty space will permit fewer weeds to take root, and that will be a huge bonus. I continue to look at garden catalogs and dream of what could be. I consider planting moonflowers along the path edge and letting them climb up the deck railings. We could watch the flowers open each evening as we finish our dinner. Dream, dream, dream.

November 2005: Thank you, Father, for a wonderful Thanksgiving Day spent at my son Gary and his wife Suzy's house. We gathered about 1:00 P.M., everyone bringing their culinary creations. Friends of Gary and Suzy, Billy and his wife Camille were visiting for the weekend with the kids, and had started their day about 3:00 A.M. for the trip to Sumner. Camille helped Suzy put in the turkey, create the green bean dish, mashed sweet potatoes, doctored them with butter and marshmallow cream, and put them in to bake. She mashed the potatoes, too. Whatever would we have done without her? Billy kept us laughing all during dinner.

Marlene had prepared several desserts. Between her and Suzy, I can't imagine a favorite that wasn't there. Suzy created a chocolate meringue pie and put it on the deck to cool, unwittingly supplying a visiting chipmunk with our Thanksgiving treat; he ate several holes in the meringue and left the chocolate undisturbed, except possibly for a few licks.

Billy decided to enjoy it anyway. Suzy, being very reluctant to serve it and its rabid possibilities, labeled it the "last resort pie," but that didn't stop Billy. At his direction his obedient wife Camille very carefully scraped meringue from the obviously affected areas, and served up a *very* small piece of the tainted pie to her husband.

Is Billy addicted to chocolate, or what?

All during dinner, Vern and Marlene kept a close check on the chipmunks who apparently thought their whole family should have had pie for Thanksgiving. One of our brightest family members conjectured about what the teenage chipmunks were probably saying in their father's hearing. After all, he had promised and then couldn't deliver.

Ah life!

Secrets of the Secret Garden

Our anticipation moved us speedily through months of waiting. We waited for the night of our grandson's performance as Archibald the Uncle in Ballard High School's performance of *The Secret Garden.*

CJ has made us proud. He participated in many music groups at Ballard High, and was an important figure on the football team. We'd watched him several times in musical/drama productions such as *Guys and Dolls*, *West Side Story*, and *High School Musical*. Each performance demonstrated his obvious growth in stage presence, character development, and voice performance. We waited impatiently for *The Secret Garden.*

On Wednesday the week of the production's first performance, I realized suddenly that I wasn't ready to see Secret Garden on stage. I'd read the book sometime, somewhere back in my history, but had very scant memories of the story. I remembered the garden and bits about the miracle that had taken place there, but nothing about the Uncle. So I drove to town to visit the library and bring the book home with me. Feeling not guilty at all, because I needed rest to get

33

rid of my cold, I read for two days and finished the book before we started for Seattle on Friday night. In spite of my freshened acquaintance with the story, I could not guess how the role of Uncle could give CJ much of a platform to display his talents.

The stage production, as did the book, began in India where a spoiled little girl named Mary had just lost her parents to a plague of Cholera. The adults in her life, knowing enough about her family to know she had an uncle in England, arranged for her travel to a strange place, a strange house, and a strange Uncle.

She is warned in various ways about the queerness of the house to which she is going and the occupants of it, and arrives to find that her uncle does not want to see her. She is shown directly to her room where she meets Martha who is to serve her.

Martha teaches her much, including how to dress herself, an activity here-to-for delegated to her servant. Martha challenges Mary to go outside and explore the Moor, a wild and wonderful neighbor to the house. Mary finally accepts her challenge, having nothing else to do.

Her Uncle Archibald, she learns, is grieving the death of his wife Lily, and has been thus occupied for nearly ten years, coming and going, but mostly avoiding his home where memories of his Lily render him sick with grief.

Mary hears strange crying in the halls where she has been forbidden to go, and is eventually drawn to disobey, thus discovering Colin, the invalid son who has been cared for by servants and neglected by his father since his mother died giving him life. Colin, here-to-for a prisoner of his thoughts, imaginations, and fears, likes Mary, and their visits become regular and expected in the household. Colin's temper tantrums decrease; the servants notice and remark.

Mary, in her wanderings outside, meets Ben Weatherford the gardener, one who has been around for many years. Ben shares tidbits about the family and discloses the existence of a special garden; a garden which has been locked up for ten years; a garden that Lily had loved. Mary is intrigued by the tale of the mysterious garden. She wants to see it. She wanders the outside garden pathways until she thinks she knows the location of the locked garden.

By this time she knows the Robin; Ben introduced him to her, and Mary begins to think Robin likes her.

Wandering the paths near the woods, Mary meets Dicken, Martha's brother; a boy who seems to be friends with all the wild animals and birds.

Robin helps Mary find the key to the garden. Mary searches near the key's hiding place for the gate and finds it overgrown with ivy and hidden from view.

Wondrous miracles happened in that Secret Garden.

Mary shared her secret cautiously with Dicken, then Colin, as she learned she could trust them. The children spent their days in the garden; Colin, being wheeled out in his chair, and then taken by Mary and Dicken into the secret place. Their thoughts were filled with the wonder of bringing the garden back to life. Dicken had so much to teach them.

Mary began to see people as friends instead of enemies. There was no longer room for anger at the world, fear of disability or fear of death. Mary and Colin grew hungry for their food and put on weight.

Colin began to dream of living instead of fearing his death and deformity. He gained the courage to stand on his feet. He dreamed of the day his dad would return. Colin would surprise him in his library by walking in unannounced. He looked forward to seeing admiration in his father's eyes instead of the pain he had always seen. They would all enjoy the garden together.

Writers of the book and the stage musical chose to emphasize different parts of this story. Where the book emphasized the children and their experiences, the stage production zeroes in on Archibald's pain and loss. It uses flashbacks and dreams to bring his relationship with Lily to the forefront. Thus, our grandson, CJ had many opportunities to sing, develop his character and convince fans. We were thrilled.

The stage production emphasizes the adult relationships rather than the children's while still bringing us to the same wonderful end.

Colin learns to walk.

His father is drawn home by his own epiphany with nature to learn Colin's secret. He realizes that he has reason to stay home and be involved, that he has a life there with his son, and Mary has become an important part of it.

This story strongly emphasizes the healing power of being outside in creation, seeing its resurrection in spring, participating in its restoration. Being in the presence of nature and seeing God working, called magic in this story, brings positive thoughts into one's mind and heart, thus crowding out the negative images which move our lives in adverse ways.

What a wonderful way to spend an evening! I wish we could do it again.

Spring Visitor

The following poem is a tetractys. It starts with one syllable, increases one syllable each line till line five. Line five is ten syllables. Second verse starts with ten syllables, then decreasing syllables each line, 4, 3, 2, 1. Enjoy the picture with me.

Spring
Robin
Redbreast comes
Hopping, pecking,
Flying to and fro, sitting 'midst crocus
Searching worm's movement; filling babies'
mouths.
Gard'ners watching
Welcome spring,
Rejoice,
Smile.

Garden Diary, 2006

March 2006: I haven't watched one movie since we lost Mom in early January. I'm not sure why. It doesn't seem like an interesting thing to do any more.

I have been out in the yard a couple of times this week; spotted all these little Maple seeds sticking up out of the grass, just as eager to grow as can be. First I thought I would rake them, but about two minutes of that convinced me it was not the way to go. Then I decided I should mow the lawn and hope to get rid of at least some of them. I mowed the lawn; now we'll see how it worked.

I'm not in very good shape! I've not been doing much physically except at work where I do a lot of walking back and forth to the office. I'm going to ease into all the garden work. My garden spot that I've been building is going to be difficult to deal with. I made a mistake and put the hydrangea trimmings in the compost pile last fall. I discovered yesterday that they are all growing. That was not the plan! They are too tough to cut with the spade, so it looks like I will have to dig them all out and *there are a lot of pieces!* Live and learn. If I had the energy, I would pot the little hydrangeas and take them to school for the plant sale in the later spring. Somehow, I doubt I'll get it done.

Thankfully I had enough sense not to put the rose trimmings into compost, too.

March 2006: Sara and Sue from Fellowship church of Christ in Seattle came all the way to Buckley to visit me on Thursday evening. They took me to dinner at the Thai food restaurant. I had been feeling dizzy all day and really didn't feel like eating, but their visit really encouraged me. They brought a plant for my garden, a dark purple winter-blooming Hellebore in bloom, so every year in March the memory and the plant will bless me. I'm thinking of putting it right by the front door where we'll see it often and up-close.

April 2006: The garden is coming along. Some of the tulips are blooming now. They are so beautiful, and I will always want more than I have. I guess that's one reason they say a garden is an on-going development.

The lilacs are blooming in Seattle, and I think I saw some in Auburn. My two little plants won't bloom this year, but someday they will be beautiful. Lilacs are absolutely wonderful. They have such a captivating scent.

The berm in the back is beginning to color up. The white rock-cress and the creeping phlox are beginning to bloom, as are many other little ground cover plants of which I can't remember names. The flowering cherry tree in the back yard is beginning to bloom. The blooms are a wonderful pink, beginning at the ends of the branches, and moving upward. When the tree is more mature, they will cover the branches! The clematis are growing strongly and putting on buds.

Spring is a wonderful time, with so much to anticipate all around us. Resurrection is everywhere, reminding us of the power of our wonderful God. He can and will also resurrect us from our weakness, and even make us strong, some glad day. Even now, He can show a few beautiful blooms in our lives. What a garden we have to imagine!

In my earthly garden I am looking forward to: seeing the Flowering Almond bush in all its glory; seeing the Sweet-William Dick and Patty shared with me bloom in my garden; seeing my tree Peony and all the different kinds of Hydrangeas I have planted developed and in bloom, hoping someday my garden will be full and rewarding.

I also dare to hope that somehow, the garden of my life will be beautiful to my Heavenly Father.

May 2006: I bought a Spirea bush last summer at a nursery in town. I wanted it because it is a plant that makes me think of Mom. She had a Spirea in our front yard while I was growing up. Mom's bush was white with heavy drooping branches when filled with bloom.

I'll never forget the red Geranium that completely filled our living-room window, either.

Winter White

The snow falls,
Huge flakes of winter white cover my walks.
The trees bloom with white tufts,
Fences announce the weight and deepness they carry.

Winter jewels adorn tiny blooming iris,
Buds on roses, blooming heather and crocus,
Emerging spring hidden beneath a blanket of white.

Gifts from My Garden

"Mom, why do you have such a large garden anyway? The work is hard and hot. Why do you do it?"

Why do I have a garden? The answer to my fifty-year-old son's question isn't short. I must share in intimate detail the rewards that come in their own time and of their own accord.

Entries from my journals help tell the story.

"During the night I was restless. Finally I arose and wandered into the living room. As I glanced into the night I saw the luminescence of my fragrant white lily, bountifully in bloom. I was deeply impressed. Later, as I went about my tasks, I thought about the picture I had seen, the light in the darkness. As I remembered the lily's beautiful fragrance, I recalled a song about Jesus. He is the Lily of the Valley. Like my lily, He stands tall, first among men. He is God. Like my lily, He lends lovely fragrance to our rather humdrum lives. Like my lily, He is beautiful, worthy to be admired, an inspiration for mortals. Like my lily,

43

He is light for our lives as we walk in this world of tears and pain."

For many years I have found comfort and release in my garden, and many times have written my joy. My sister, Mona stimulated my journaling with her support and inspiration.

"I brought you a present, Margie, several presents," she said one day about fifteen years ago. Her mischievous smile warmed me. *"I was just looking around my house and I found these. They had your name on them."* She handed me eight blank journals, including one with a teddy bear on the cover. *"This is your Bear Hug Journal,"* she said. *"Write the things that make you happy and be thankful for what you have."*

I have written my thankfulness:

"Winter is visiting again this morning. My thermometer beyond the window reads thirty-two degrees Fahrenheit, but it is much colder. Frost lies like a silver blanket over the grass, the mountains of blackberry vines in our back woods, the red barberry bush standing in solitary splendor. God uses frost to put my garden to sleep. I, too, need a rest. Frost's icy blanket turns the leaves of my Popcorn Viburnum a dark beautiful red. The new flowering cherry tree shouts at me in glorious vibrant orange. 'Good night. Good night.'"

As I study the gardening catalogues:
"I am amazed at the infinite varieties of wonderful plants and flowers. I love creating my garden. But there is so much to choose from! I find myself making lists and filling out order blanks and wanting to see and touch everything pictured in the catalogues. I love the lilies, the rhododendrons, the tulips and daffodils that bloom so early in the spring."

Another winter entry:
"Thank You, Father for giving us such excitement and so many beautiful colors and forms. I am amazed, but nothing is a wonder to You. You created the Garden of Eden, the most beautiful garden of all."

I received a nice surprise one December:
"Yesterday I saw Spring coming. We were in Seattle, and the bulbs were beginning to peek through the ground, the camellias were capering tentatively on their bushes. I was encouraged and entranced."
"Thank You, Father, for Resurrection. I enjoyed the frost-painted landscapes, but I'm looking forward to the coming of the green!"

Another May arrived at last:

45

"What a picture! The Popcorn Vibernum is in full bloom, and the neighbor's red rhododendron snuggling next to it is rejoicing, too."

I saw the first blooms the day Clio, my husband, entered the hospital with pneumonia. A whole month later, the blooms waited to welcome him home.

Would anyone like to visit my garden?
"The daylilies are opening, new ones every day. The blooms are large and lovely; orange, gold, red. I can hardly wait until there are dozens, someday. I would love to share them with you."

August's rewards:
"The phlox are so delightful. I pondered a lot before I ordered them. I was afraid the stalks might not support the weight of the blooms. I needn't have worried. They have been blooming for weeks, all shades of pink, red, and white, too; bountiful blooms greet us when we look out our bedroom window."

"The wild blackberries are ripening, plump and pretty. I look forward to putting a few in the freezer. They make my tropical jello extra tasty. I want to freeze some of that exuberant zucchini for bread at Thanksgiving time."

"I took a bouquet of fragrant Stargazer lilies to church this morning. What a joy to share them. They went home with Amy."

And then comes the harvest:

"Yesterday was Labor Day, so this lady acted appropriately and labored in the garden. The vegetables and berries invited, 'Eat me, Eat me!'"

"The squash harvest was prolific: The extras went into a box. Desperate phone calls went to neighbors whether we knew them or not. Success! One neighbor offered to take the whole box!"

"The blackberries hung heavy on the vines. I picked a gallon and put them in the freezer. The beans filled a big kettle; they and the strawberries embellished our dinner."

"These small labors reminded me of the harvests You bring faithfully to those who plant, tend and reap, Lord. Thank You for giving us your bounty."

More journal reflections:

"The garden encourages creativity. The garden provides respite and restoration to the weary of heart. The garden blesses the earth and brings joy to men. What a gift is a garden!"

Why do I want a garden? Don't you see, my son? It is the garden that makes me rich.

Celebration of God's Love

The flowers have color. The birds can sing.
The grass is green, and fresh, and spring
Awakens all these joys to me.
Shall I forget to thankful be
To God above, Who let me see?

He didn't have to color earth
When He gave His creation birth.
He wanted me to feel His love
And so, He put blue skies above
And colored everything I see
With beauties of His Love for me.

So if you ever doubt the love
Of your Most Powerful God above,
Just look around at all you see
And hear Him say, "My child, for thee."

Holey Moley Desperation

At Christmas time this year we had one of the best snowfalls of our seven-year history in Golden Valley, Buckley, Washington. The 'White Christmas' resulting was the stuff fairy tales are made of, and lingered for several weeks, transforming our woodland setting to a dazzling show of frosty wintry white. From the safety and warmth of our family room we gazed, wondering at the beauty of the change God had wrought in our own back yard.

One morning during my leisurely inspection of our winter wonderland, I was jolted into reality. Under the snow in the middle of the lawn, Mt. Vesuvius was rising! This sight brought consternation and realization. The moles were busy, even in the middle of winter, even under four inches of snow! What an unwelcome sight, destroying my peace of mind and growing my guilt over work that I wasn't doing in the garden. It was winter, after all!

Moles, a common pest in the Northwest, drive most gardeners to near-neuroses, as evidenced by the number of remedies on sale at the hardware store,

49

written up in gardening magazines, and passed by word-of-mouth by anyone who has found 'the answer' to the destruction they cause.

Our friend, Bob, was the first to attempt our rescue from the pesky little varmints that pushed up mounds, continued along my brick-lined beds evicting bricks from their hard-won homes, creating a mess impossible to repair, and uprooting any plant unfortunate enough to be in their path. Then they wreaked their havoc in my beautiful green lawn.

When Bob couldn't abide the mess in our front yard any longer, he went to the hardware store and bought a generous supply of smoke bombs. In order to use the bombs he had to dig down into the mound, find the direction the mole had gone, and send the smoke into the actual run.

As he demonstrated the process: one lights the fuse, hurriedly sticks the bomb down into the run, frantically tries to cover it with dirt, and runs, hoping not to gas oneself along with the mole. Several sessions of smoke bombing later–after which the moles were usually excited into increased frantic activity–Bob had another idea.

This time he brought along his wife's hair dryer. After hooking it to electricity, digging into the moles' run and inserting the bomb, turned it on, thinking he would make this long story short. The hair dryer moved the smoke through the runs, all right, as evidenced by the geysers of smoke arising all over our yard, and over at the neighbors! However we saw no evidence that the moles were bothered. Instead, we heard in our heart of hearts the moles asking one another, "Have you tried that new flavor of tobacco? They were giving free samples today. Did you miss it?"

Eventually, doing my garden shopping and reading, I discovered a product called a Mole Chaser. Hopefully, I ordered two of them–front and back yards both displayed bountiful evidence of the moles' presence. This miracle of someone's imagination was supposed to send out vibrations which moles hate; consequently, the moles would just stay out of your yard. Sounded good.

Directions were to bury the Mole Chaser upright; that meant a considerable amount of digging through our rocky soil...no small job; the device was about a foot tall.

The magic didn't work in our yard. The moles snuggled close, reporting to their peers, "They've put in two new massage parlors! Check them out."

The batteries died, and I forgot where I buried my Mole Chasers; they are now trying vainly to compost in their eternal home.

My daughter sent me a remedy suggested to her by a frustrated gardener behind prison bars. The lady told her she had gone to a golf course where she had never seen any evidence of moles. The gardener had told her the secret was to bury broken glass in the mole runs.

I hurried out to insert seltzer bottles into the runs, broke them with my crow bar, and waited, feeling very smug about my new knowledge. The theory was if moles cut themselves they won't heal, but will bleed to death. If my seltzer bottles murdered any moles, I never knew it. What I did see, over and over again, was a new mound where the old one had been. These new mounds stood, brazenly decorated with broken glass, now on the surface in my lawn, as if those moles were taunting me. "Ha! Ha! Ha! Fooled you again!"

Another trick I actually tried I found in a garden circular. It stated Juicy Fruit Gum was very popular among moles. It *must* be Juicy Fruit. The theory here was when the mole tried to eat the gum it would become stuck in his digestive system and he would die.

I went into my yard and garden armed with a large package of *the* gum. As with every other mole-chasing tactic, I had to dig down into the mole run. Then I un-wrapped the gum, chewed it, and threw it into the run along with mole poison and covered it all with dirt. The moles must be wearing new gum-balls on their noses, or blowing bubbles with the gum. They still romp nonchalantly through my garden.

My neighbors finally took pity on me. (Anyone who would believe all *that* was seriously in need of help!) My next-door-neighbor, Dick, came over with his scissor traps. He set them repeatedly; the moles must have misunderstood the purpose of the traps. Perhaps they thought them some kind of puzzle to play with, or in. Only one of my resident moles met his Maker through Dick's traps, even though Dick was diligent about covering each trap with a bucket to keep out all the light.

Tom was the most skillful trapper. There was a difference in the way he set the traps; after the trap was in the run he would be sure to put dirt back into the run on either side of the trap to hide it from the moles. And he wore gloves. Thanks to Tom I have two or three fewer moles to make my life difficult.

But the moles still come, and I continue to search on and on looking for the perfect way to escape this holey moley desperation.

Gardener's Lament

I wandered out toward the wetland
To get rid of my kitchen scraps.
Compost Tumbler awaits me there,
Its belly feeling gaps.
Deer track I spotted
Sharing plant's bed.
Plants chomped off,
Flowers
Dead.

Author's Note: Well, they're probably not *dead*, but severely set back. Wetland borders our property. This poem is a Nonet, a poem of nine lines, beginning with the first line which has nine syllables, each succeeding line has one less syllable. The last line has one. No rhyme needed. I just wanted it to rhyme.

Friendly Flowers

Friendly flowers,
Up-turned faces
Smiling gently
Oh, so sweetly
Quietly they cheer me on

Vibrant beauty
Vanish greyness
Standing nobly
In humble places
Asking not a glorious throne

Singing sweetly
Heaven's kindness
Singing softly
Wondrous love
Calling upward spirit's essence
Gifting mortals
Gentle Love

Mona Armas
February 4, 1994

Mona Armas is my dear sister. I'm so proud of who she is and what she has written.

Procrastination

My garden waits for me.
I linger longer, putting thoughts
on paper. Sun shines on.
Day is gone. I write.

Oops! No Harvest!

They said today I should plant my peas,
Those gard'ners who know what is right.
Point their fingers sharp at me
As if they knew my plight.

Procrastination, it imprisons,
Keeps me in my chair.
Writer's thoughts predominate;
Gardening error.

The Teaching of a Tulip

Tulip
You speak deeply
You comfort me
Your brilliant beauty drew me close
My spirit leaped for joy
Your bloom eagerly awaited
Those cold, grey days of March

On that bright spring day
Sun-Light prevailed
I learned from you
Eternal Truth

.

You open your deepest heart
To the warmth of the Sun
To reveal secrets
Of black and gold
I am like you

In the warm presence of the Son
I reach upward, I reach outward
I open my carefully protected depths
To revel in His Love

By Mona Armas

Birthday Gift from God

I look around my garden in my birthday month of May
And marvel at the beauty it displays.
I see my big Viburnum tree, Popcorn is its name
Covered with white clusters, shouting grace.

Red Rhododendron crowds so close contributing its
share
Of glory to the picture that I see.
Blue Iris swell and stretch their splendor far into the
air
And then reflect their radiance back to me

So many gifts I see and love, the rose azaleas from
above
Spread beneath my window full and free.
Pink Tulips, Rose, blue Violets, expressions of His
love
Among the gifts my Father gives to me.

Thank you, Glorious Father for gifting me your care
For sending warmth and rain, the sun and light
For every flow'r you send to me, each one that shines
so fair
Shares extra ways you show your power and might.

June Morning

Rain falls softly from leaden skies
On lawns, gardens, woods, nourishing them.

The bird calls fewer and quieter this morning;
The lone adventurer darts across my backyard sky.

I drink in the moment, savoring each color, shape, and
sound.

I sip my coffee, hot and sweet, taking it all in,
Enjoying God's gifts: life, beauty, another morning.

Flowers that bloom: tall spikes of red hot poker still
reaching, orange and yellow,
My new purple-white delphinium, two blooms, short,
fresh from the nursery,

Bright gold and red marigolds, branching,
Surviving the munching of deer and rabbits.
Daylily's spikes filled with promise of color-
explosions,
Filling me with anticipation.

Wild flowers, the Foxglove, pink and white, here and
there, bonus flowers I did not plant.

A lone deep purple iris among white blossoms of
yarrow, making me wish I'd planted them more
carefully and increased their bounty; I resolve to fix
my error before another year passes.

Then comes a realization. I have but today, this
minute, this hour.
I am richly blessed to witness these tokens of God's
love and faithfulness.
What will I do with these precious moments I have
received?

Tulip

Standing straight and tall
Waiting for the moment
When Light calls forth
Your hidden beauty

Not by force or power
But by the warming presence
Your inner secrets
Are called forth
For those with eyes to see

At your point of deepest opening
Is your time of deepest giving
You yield your petals back to earth
Yielding in trust
To the promise of eternity
That
What dies in one form
Will come again
In New Life

By Mona Armas

Geraniums and Petunias

Our family comes from a long line of Helpful Harries. Family personality resemblances are often a source of amusement and pleasure to family members as well as acquaintances of our family.

In order to illustrate our type of helpfulness I'll tell you of a recent visit to my home when my sister, Mona, brought a gift; not just one journal, but eight journals, to help me work through a significant problem in my life. One of the journals was to be a Bear-Hug Journal where I was to record the happy events, memories, and thoughts of my life.

The first wonderful memory I recorded in the Bear-Hug Journal told of the snack run to the grocery store we made that day. Mona and I went to the Bi Mart down the street looking for satisfactions for our sweet-tooth.

As we approached the front of the store, we stopped to admire the garden plants on display. We met there a young man who was acting somewhat lost, and who said he was doing some shopping for his wife. He asked us if we knew anything about flowers.

We certainly did! For the next twenty minutes we regaled him with *everything* we knew about geraniums and petunias.

"Geraniums and Petunias are annuals. Does your wife want annuals or perennials? How tall does she want the plant to be? Does she want to plant it in sun or shade?"

Later we decided we had dumped the whole load of hay on the cow. We figured this out when we saw the young recipient of our wisdom going home *without* buying geraniums, petunias, or pansies. He took home only a tall story about two older ladies who sure liked to talk and helped only to confuse him.

Lesson learned: Too much helpfulness is no help at all!

Ode to Red Robin Rose

Red Robin blooms before my glass,
And as I pass
Still I see more
Outside my door.
Red rose blooming in my front yard,
I work so hard.
The rose adorns
And I trim thorns.

Is it worth the time I spend?
Or does it lend
Without an end;
Enrich my life?

Oh yes, it does. It gives me more.
The joy I store
Lasts on and on
Till winter's gone.

Entranced

I looked through my window toward the wood.
On my berm like statues stood
Two deer entranced by seeing me.
I looked right back with mounting glee
At those two deer entranced by me.

One doe remained like statue still,
Not moving hoof, nor ear, nor tail,
Declining food. Our eyes did meet.
The other bowed its head to eat
St. Johnswort growing round its feet.

The eater wandered on to find
Another bite. I'm not inclined
To let her bite another flower
Or watch her for another hour
Grazing here within my bower.

I wave my arms to show my power,
I snap my dishtowel. Do they cower?
Oh no. They stand, entranced by me,
Wonder next what they will see;
Refuse to let my bower be.

Calla Lily

Calla Lily, tall and white
Tell me why you shine so bright
Reaching for the stars, it seems
Or is it for the bright moonbeams?

Or do you reach for up above
To bask within Creator's Love;
Escape the darkness of the ground
Where bulbs lie hidden, earthen bound?

You shine to bless us in your season
Then fade away, what is the reason?
Beauty such as yours should be
Ever here for us to see.

I wonder why huge leaves that shine
Keep reaching up, so tall, so fine,
Then fall down, spent, though heaven bound.
In disappointment on the ground.

The very reaching brought your fall
And now you lie in mounding pall.
It's time to grace a glad bouquet
And try to make somebody's day.

Again, you're standing straight and tall
And bless my household, one and all.
Pink clusters keep you company.
Rejoice in happy jubilee.

Thank you, Calla Lily.

Daylily Lunch

Late afternoon, and I'd come in
To tackle dinner once again.
When I looked out, what did I see
But a doe; she was dining voraciously.
She ate one daylily, then she ate two,
And reached for another; What did I do?

I walked outside; said imperiously,
"What do you think you're doing to me?"
She raised her head, and yet she stood
As if saying to me, "This flower's good."
She stayed there as long as she thought she could
And then ambled off into the wood.

Evening Song

Weary with day's efforts I go to my bed, eyes exhausted from peering at book pages and computer screens.

I glance through the open window at my summer garden and am captivated by the gifts of God so gloriously combined into my landscape.

Just outside my window, Azalea bush still clings to the bountiful bloom she gave. Next to her, the Phlox stretch still higher, hurrying to remind me of last year's glory.
The meandering border of the outside garden beckons my eyes to the end.

I see Popcorn Viburnum, Flowering Plum, Hydrangea, and then huge heart-shaped shining Hosta—leaf-centers white, bordered green—commands my attention. Among my other plants she glows like the queen she is.

I am loath to close the window and shut out the garden.

It is You I feel, God, here among Your beautiful creations, and You speak peace.

I lie on my bed, windows and blinds still open, wanting to be near You, and I know once again how very beautiful Eden, the home You prepared for man, must have been.

***

My heart sings "The earth is full of Your glory;
it comes to me every day,
As I willingly follow Your footsteps
to walk in the heavenly way."

Eventide

As shadows of the evening outside my window fall
I look into my garden and hear my Father's call.
Come Child, I am waiting to walk and talk with you.
I know you need to be with me and feel my love for you.

You've struggled through another day, climbed yet another height,
Your heart is heavy, weighted down; you're weary of the fight.
Just lie down now upon your bed, be still and know I'm God;
I'm with you here, please understand I walk upon this sod.

I see your struggles every day; I know and feel your pain.
I hear your heart cry out to Me for strength to try again.

I know you're trying to believe; you see your guilt and sin.
Remember Child, I died for you, no matter where you've been.

Keep your eyes turned toward Me, and not upon your sin

Then I can change your heart and life, My battle I can
win.
I love you Child, delight in you each time you seek My
face.
Someday you'll meet your Savior, you'll be like Him
by His Grace.

*Beloved, now we are children of God, and
it has not appeared as yet what we shall
be. We know that, when He appears, we
shall be like Him, because we shall see
Him just as He is.*
I John 3:2-3

Butterfly

Imagine you're a collector for The Butterfly House at Pacific Science Center in Seattle.

You've gone to Latin America to collect a Blue Morpho Butterfly from the tropical forests. You know if you see one flying it will be a miracle—adult Blue Morphos usually hide on the forest floor, wings folded above their heads, camouflaged by the neutral brown colors of their wings' undersides.

This butterfly is most sought after. You do *not* want to return home without it.

You trudge through the forest all day without seeing the treasure you seek. Without warning the recognizable bright blue metallic wings appear and disappear ahead.

Cautiously you sit down, deciding to study the butterfly's habits while you eat lunch. Then you'll pursue your prize. You watch him flutter from flower to flower while you think about how nice it will be to own this specimen and take it home for the Butterfly House collection. You doze off. When you awake the butterfly is gone.

***

Now let's look at today's reality. What is the butterfly you're planning to capture?

You love your parents and grandparents. You intend to spend more time with them; to listen to and record stories of the lives they lived; to ask them all the questions you thought of at inconvenient times. Your intentions are to honor your elders. You make plans to visit your grandparents, but your friends want to get together at the arranged time, or you have to work the weekend, or the church is having a social that same weekend. You put the visit off knowing they will understand and still love you. Time passes on. Your loved ones grow older. You realize time is getting short, and still want to bring them to your home and get out the tape recorder, but life gets in the way.

Months and years slide by.

One day time runs out. Your father breathes his last. You have memories, but nagging regrets, too. So many of his days are lost forever to you now. You could have asked how it felt to design a highway and see it after completion. You could have asked what he did on the day you were born. You could have asked whether he liked school at age twelve or who was his favorite teacher and why. The opportunity is lost forever.

Life happens in a way that makes it far too easy to put last things first and first things last. Show your loved ones how you cherish them and want to spend time with them. Give away those hugs you've been storing. Write down a note to cherish a memory. Save your parents' story. Pack your treasure chest full.

Don't be lulled into thinking you have lots of time. The only time you can know you possess is this minute.

Don't let the beautiful butterfly of memory escape while you sleep.

The butterfly won't linger long.

Audacious Visitor

A deer came visiting today,
Out of the woods she did sashay.
But did she knock upon my door?
Oh no, she stopped a step before
And dined on my tomato vine
I'd put so close
Cause it was mine.

I wanted her to stay away.
But she came visiting today.
Right up my walk she boldly pranced
It would appear she even danced
Right up to my tomato vine.
She didn't care that it was mine.

Against the house it stood so tall
And green tomatoes covered all
Awaiting sunshine's ripening power
And my arrival in the bower.
She ate and ate not leaving one,
And when I came they all were gone.

In vain I kept them close to me
Where I could see she left them be.
She sneaked in at the midnight hour
And had her feast, despite the sour.
She ate and ate not leaving one
And when I came they all were gone.

Blackberry Feast

While looking out at the woodland
I saw a couple of deer
That moseyed into my vision
Just a few short feet from here.

They didn't look at all at me
They're focused on some food.
At least they're not eating my garden
As any good deer should.

Instead they're nonchalantly eating
wild blackberries out of the patch,
Ignoring those scratchy thorny vines
Consuming a good-sized batch.

When I go there to pick a few
To maybe make some jam
Those thorns just poke and scratch my skin
Until I finally scram.

Those deer ate on ten minutes or so
Ne'er noticing all those stickers
While I come in the house all scratched
And have to change my knickers.

It doesn't seem at all quite fair
When I think about it;
That they should nonchalantly graze
Where I get stuck and shout it.

The deer don't wash or can or save
The berries, they just eat em;
Don't worry 'bout the dirt or rave
Then walk away and leave'em.

Gardener Imitating God

And He (Jesus) came to Nazareth, where He had been brought up, and as was His custom, He entered the synagogue on the Sabbath, and stood up to read. And the book of the prophet Isaiah was handed to Him. And He opened the book, and found the place where it was written. "The Spirit of the Lord is upon Me, Because He anointed Me to preach the gospel to the poor, He has sent Me to proclaim release to the captives, And recovery of sight to the blind, to set free those who are downtrodden, to proclaim the favorable year of the Lord." And he closed the book, and gave it back to the attendant, and sat down; and the eyes of all in the synagogue were fixed upon Him. And He began to say to them, "Today this Scripture has been fulfilled in your hearing."
Luke 4:16-21

I planted the tree as a twig shortly after we moved to our new home in 2002. It was a flowering variety, I knew, but as yet it had never bloomed to inform me of what bloom it would bear. The

81

identification key the Arbor Society had sent failed miserably and left room for much doubt and confusion, so I failed to name my tree. But I loved it as it grew in my yard for the next three years.

In December of 2005 the tree had grown to seven or eight feet tall. It was the largest and most beautiful of the tiny trees-grown-up that I had planted. Even though winter approached, my tree still carried its bounty of colorful fall leaves.

Around Christmas we had a windstorm—not a violent one as I would judge—but as I walked through my garden I discovered my tree lying wounded, trunk split vertically to the ground, bark torn, mortally wounded, I thought. Disconsolate, I left it on the ground and went inside. Later that afternoon, drawn by the plight of my tree, I went back for another look. I discovered hope.

The broken branches of the tree clung tenaciously to life by bark and under-tissue. Immediately I regretted having left it exposed to the weather all day. Perhaps with some help it could have been healed, I thought, and went inside to bed. I could not rest. I could not give up so easily on my beautiful tree. I had never seen the blooms yet!

Bright and early the next morning I went to my tree again. God has put amazing tenacity in growing things, I thought. I'm going to do my best to save this tree.

82

I found some tree-supports in my front yard. Judging that they were no longer needed by the flowering plum trees, I appropriated them to my project. I looked for more materials to bind the split trunk together, the fallen portion to the standing portion. I propped and tied and pried until the tree was again upright. And then I prayed for a miracle. And I received it.

The tree stood in its bandages for several years until it healed. Today it stands, independent of all exterior supports. But I still don't know its name and haven't seen its bloom. Still I wait.

In all these imperfect rescue-efforts I was but imitating my Heavenly Father. We are described as God's Vineyard. Jesus, the Messiah, came to "bind up the broken-hearted, give a garland for ashes." His purpose is stated: "So they will be called Oaks of Righteousness, the planting of the Lord, that He may be glorified." God knows the wonderful intentions he has for us. Our name has been given. We are "Oaks of Righteousness" standing in uprightness and trust for our Savior.

Will not the Father of us all, the Heavenly Gardener, be able to bind our wounds as he stated? Will He not give us a garland of flowers in place of our abundance of ashes? Will He sleep unconcernedly while we weep?

Because the Lord has anointed me to bring good news to the afflicted, to bind up the broken-hearted ..."giving them a garland instead of ashes, so they will be called oaks of righteousness, the planting of the Lord that He may be glorified.
Isaiah 61:1

November

How can it be November? Already! It's the time of red and gold, lingering greens and bright oranges, all shouting in chorus, "See me now, while I'm here. Remember, a long cold winter is coming." In our yard and the Learns' the Espinosa trees hold long sprays of rosy-pink blooms-turned–to- seeds, waiting to assure the continuation of copious life as well as ensure our fall raking chore is cut out for us.

The first hard frost will paint our lawns in silvery whiteness, the last leaves will fall and the trees will stand nakedly for several months, resting until Spring invites tiny lime green sprouts to her resurrection party.

Yellow-gold-green pumpkins, squash, and gourds of every size and shape join the autumn explosion of color. Wreaths, overflowing baskets, flower sprays, and scarecrows lining walls and aisles fill our senses to overflowing. We search for that last corn on the cob in the grocery stores and last zucchini in the garden.

Multicolored giant hydrangeas gifted by our dear neighbors and settled into a crystal vase, grace our coffee table. Fields of pumpkins amaze us with their bumper crops. Corn- grown-tall hides mazes trampled by uncounted Halloween ghosts and goblins.

Heart-felt thanksgiving in such a season as this comes easily. It's the time when our families gather, tell varied versions of the family past designed to make us laugh, exchange hugs, and share inspirations and accomplishments.

I sit with pen and empty sheet of paper writing the good things that fill my life. When the page can hold no more, I get another and continue my exercise in giving thanks. As I write I recognize how rich I am, and my heart lifts. I contemplate a new habit, realizing it's difficult to be depressed while I appreciate my blessings. Won't you join me?

GOD

God created us to live with him in purity, because he loved and wanted us, and wanted our love in return. He could have made us so we couldn't disobey him, but a robot can't love...love is a decision.

God gave man a choice, a decision. Everything man would do would be a choice of good or evil. Every action, decision and feeling would be a choice that would either draw man closer or separate him more from his Creator.

Man *did* make wrong decisions. Beginning with Adam's sin, man moved farther and farther away from God.

When He created man as He did, He knew that man would need a Savior from his wrong choices, his sin, his missing of God's purpose for him. So our Loving God made a plan; the only plan that could save man from his guilt and from the wages of sin: He would send His Son to earth, to live as God had wanted man to live; then He would collect the wages of man's sins by dying on the Cross.

Man could only earn the wages of sin (death). Jesus earned eternal life, yet died for man's sins. He

became sin for us. *He made Him who knew no sin to be sin on our behalf that we might become the righteousness of God in Him.*
Romans 6:23, II Corinthians 5:21

As the dirty rag in the bucket can't wash itself, even if it sits in the same room with the washing machine and laundry detergent, so we can't cleanse ourselves from sin. That is what Jesus did when he died on the cross.
Author Unknown

He Inhabits Eternity

You asked of my God...Who is He? Is He great?
Where can He be?
I know, I can tell you for certain. He inhabits eternity.

He created the world I live in. He reached down from
his throne above, and fashioned a man for His
pleasure: to be with him and live in His love.

Wanting Love, He gave man an opinion:
he might choose to love God, or no.
And to those who would willingly love Him He gave
lives with His Spirit aglow.

What a wonder! My God dwells within me!
What a blessing! He shows me my way.
How revealing! He shows me His purpose
And He giveth His strength for my day.

Every day I can live in His Presence, and I sing! How
my confidence swells,
For I know when the way grows dreary. He controls!
He does all things well.

How I wonder sometimes why He loved me; how so great a marvel could be,
That My God though so great, should desire me...living with Him in eternity!
Written for a neighbor in Olympia

The Storm

A storm passed by;
Bitter cold, heavy snow, freezing rain.
Each leaf, twig, stalk and blade
bowed to the ground, entombed in ice.

Usually silent woods hold a cacophony of sound:
Crack! Sound of branch splitting,
Falling noises, iced leaves, twigs and branches
Crash!

Again and again, over here, over there,
I look, straining to see where, which tree has broken;
Which is no longer reaching for the sky,
Which will be next?

I grieve. Topless trees stand
embarrassed by their lack of finesse.
Trunks endure, uselessly supporting
lost branches by bark alone.

Here a tree, there a tree, now leaning
Tempted to the ground or sky.

91

Will it fall next windstorm? Or
Will it continue its courageous
reach, roots clinging tenaciously?

So am I, wounded by unexpected ice,
Broken by a critical word,
Hurting from scars inflicted long ago.
I'd rather be whole, beautiful, perfect,
But I cling, sink my roots deep into the
Soil of God's wonderful love,
And I stand.

Sense-i-cal Winter

Peering out my winter window, I see white everywhere: the lawn, frozen in a layer of ice; fir branches enclosed in an icy tomb; flowering plum branches bowing to the ground with their icy weight.

I venture through my front door and see my breath flowing white as I converse with my husband. I look back at the house and see heavy icicles hanging along the eaves, tempting me to touch, and when I do my fingers stick. I push and the icy spears come crashing down in a cacophony of sound.

The icy air cools, and then prickles my skin. Each breath clasps my nostrils in an icy hug.

Suddenly a new sharp sound makes me jump; another tree in the woods has cracked and fallen, wounded by Washington's winter leaping in like a lion.

I flee into the house. Warmth embraces me. I rejoice to see the fall colors still decorating my living room. Piano music, gifted by a friend, welcomes me in; aromas of chocolate and sweetness enfold me. I feel comforted. I sample the cookies and taste my favorite chocolate chips melted in a chewy warm treat. I am content.

Whimsical Winter

I couldn't believe it. The storm ended, and the deception began:

Winter tiptoes in, deceiving us, sending gentle rains to cool gardens, soothing us.
Winter breathes again, a glacial, frosty breath coating trees with ice; weighting branches to the ground; roughly wrenching boughs from trunks and throwing them onto power lines; littering yards with limbs; crashing whole trees; mutilating others.

Winter steals our lives: no reading, no hot coffee in early morning, no hot food to warm us within. We retreat to beds piled high with blankets.

Winter gifts us with neighbors long not seen, reaching out, offering warmth and food steaming hot, soup and coffee restoring us.

Winter tiptoes in, deceiving us, sending gentle rains to cool gardens, soothing us.

The Wounded Woods

Why these branches on the ground?
Why these tree-tops low?
Why the peaks of tallest trees
Lie broken in the snow?

Why the roadsides piled so high
With Nature's fitful leavings
Why my garden broken down
And leaving me here grieving?

Fallen branches everywhere
Lying in confusion
No longer ordered on the tree
Strewn in sore delusion.

My life's so like these wounded woods;
Things not what they should be.
The things I should, I cannot do,
I'm very like those trees.

Life's storms have left their mark on me
Though tired, wounded, worn,
I'll take another step and see
God's gift, another morn.

Renewal

Those wounded woods are smiling now
In spite of stormy scars
They're putting on another face;
Forgetting icy wars.

Those icy storms are in the past;
No use to grieve and fret
The broken branches on the ground;
Confusion reigning yet.

It's time they wore a face of green.
It's time that they forget
And recognize that Spring has come;
The ground is waiting, wet.

"It's time," they hear the robin call,
"Wake up, put on your clothes
Its beauty will surround you soon,
Much sooner than you know"

The robin found responsive ear
The woods put on their show
Enjoying summer's warmth and sun
Before the winter snow

I'm learning from those wounded woods:
Joy waits for me right now.
In spite of grief and loss and pain
I'll take a step somehow

The moments that I live today
Hold beauties I can see
If I'll but open up my eyes
They'll pour their joy on me

And so I'll wear a brighter face
Not drag around and grieve
Rejoice in moments through the day
And then I'll really live

With God in the Garden

There comes a bright and happy day
When you and I will pause,
Forget about the shadows, grey,
And look instead at *The Cause.*

We'll follow Spring's voice and go outside
While she's still waiting there.
We'll touch, with her, the Primrose face
And breathe her gentle air.

Behold the budding Tulip poised
And waiting for the time
When sunlight brings her forth to bloom
In splendor, so sublime.

We'll walk through Autumn's cast-off clothes
And search for the promise of
New dresses of yellow and white and rose,
Spring, wearing the Father's Love.

And when we must pick up our task,
Return to the stress and strain,
We'll take with us that Love, we'll ask,
"Can't we visit the garden again?"

For we found our Father waiting there,
His arms stretched out to cheer,

To solace, refresh, confirm His care
For us, still struggling here.

He waits there still, so let's take the time
To welcome Spring, Summer, Fall.
To immerse our souls, yes, both yours and mine
In the Love oe'r the garden wall.

The author who wrote this last entry in *Blooms, Blunders, and Blessings* is my oldest son. You might say writing runs in the family. Thank you, Doug, for making me proud.

A Ghost in the Garden

I want to write; so I tell myself on a regular basis. Unfortunately, I find myself choosing other things to do: staring at the paper, cleaning the house, visiting the ghost in the garden...

Oh yes! I have a ghost in my garden.

He greets me every evening and walks the garden with me. Together we review the day's events, evaluate each bloom, make plans for tomorrow's garden. He tells me of past gardens that grew here, of the little old lady who lived here before me...visiting the garden each morning; how she came to remember her past—the family, her children, her friends.

He tells me she grew lonely, and of how he became her daily companion. Others thought she was senile when she spoke of him, but I know...

He tells me of the day she died, alone in her old age, with no one to attend. But my ghost sat with her.

He told her of the new blooms in the garden, of the fragrant perfume of the lilac, of the heavy-burdened aroma of the lily, of the light-hearted scent of the violet.

He showed her the rush of the wind, the patter of the rain, the rich deep clean smells of the earth.

When she finally moved on, he helped her on her way, showing her the new garden in which she would dwell. He introduced her to the Master Gardener, from whom she would receive more than she could ever imagine, then, he left her content and no longer lonely...and returned to my garden.

You see, he knew I would need him. I am lonely, too; and so I walk with the ghost in my garden. He is my daily companion. We stroll among the flowers, and he enjoys their beauties with me. He loves me, and his presence soothes my pain.

Some day, I suppose I shall move on too. My ghost will share with me in my last moments the new blooms, the scents of the lilac, and the heady fragrance of the lily...

Together we will rush into the wind, through the patter of rain, leaving behind the deep, clean smell of the earth.

God's garden is a better place, with colors much brighter and scents more appealing than those in mine.

God waters my pain, and I will grow through it.

Then my ghost will return to my garden to lead yet another weary soul into the Garden of God.

Douglas L. Skelton

***

I tell you the truth; it is expedient for you that I go away: for if I go not away, the Comforter will not come unto you; but if I depart, I will send him unto you.

John 16:7
Authorized King James Version

Thank you for spending this bit of time with me. I hope you'll find much joy in your garden, and mine, as often as you wish.
God bless!

Marjorie

A Parting Thought

For since the creation of the world His (God's) invisible attributes, His eternal power and divine nature have been clearly seen, being understood through what has been made, so that they (created men) are without excuse. Romans 1:20
New American Standard Bible

Other Titles
By Marjorie Vaughn Eldred

Seizing the Treasure: 101 Nuggets to Warm
Your Heart

Journey from Addiction to Freedom
A Family's Prison Experience

Both titles available in Print and EBooks

Amazon

Made in the USA
Charleston, SC
25 July 2014